Fabulous Filli
for Baked Pota

Suitable for Vegetarians and Vegans

SABINA CHANCE

First published in Great Britain in 2005 by:
Opening Chapter, 43 Maes Road, Llanelli, SA14 8UH

www.openingchapter.com

A catalogue record for this book is available
from the British Library

ISBN 1-904958-00-1

This book is dedicated to the potato

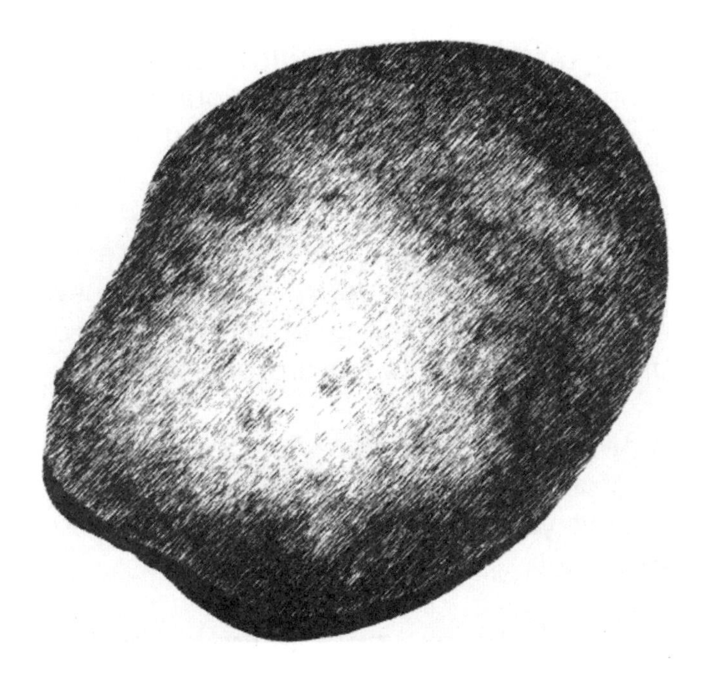

Thanks and acknowledgements

When you start the process of writing a cookery book you kid yourself into believing that your experience of the subject will see you through.

But as you get deeper into the research and the inevitable tasting sessions with family and friends, you soon discover the gaps in your knowledge and realise that you've underestimated the time and effort required to finish it.

By the time such a project is complete, you have plundered not only your own knowledge and experience but also those of everyone around you and all the recipe ideas from other sources.

It's impossible to thank everyone, so to those of you who contributed, knowingly and unknowingly - a big thank you. Special thanks to R; you know who you are.

I'd also like to thank you, the cook who has bought this book, without you it wouldn't exist. I hope you find using it as rewarding an experience as I did researching it.

Sabina Chance

CONTENTS

INTRODUCTION

Eat more fresh potatoes.

On average, people in the UK eat 110kg of potatoes each per year. That's about 2 kilograms or 4 pounds per week. Unfortunately in recent years more of this consumption has been of processed potatoes in the form of frozen chips and other potato products.

Now less than half of the potatoes eaten in the UK are bought fresh. In the United States, consumption of processed potatoes overtook the consumption of fresh potatoes more than ten years ago.

The best way to eat potatoes is with their skin on, this keeps more of their nutritional value intact, that's why baked potatoes are good for you.

It's not difficult to bake fresh potatoes, hardly more effort than going to the freezer and tipping a couple of handfuls of frozen chips into hot oil.

At its simplest, all you have to do is to clean any dirt off (and many potatoes now come pre-washed anyway) and place them in a hot oven for an hour.

Eat them with the skin on.

Don't forget to eat the skin; this is one of the most nutritious parts of a potato, see the chapter on potato nutrition for more information.

This book sets out to encourage you to eat your potatoes in their most nutritious and delicious form by presenting innovative and tasty recipes, ranging from the easy to prepare lunchtime snack to recipes suitable for the most demanding dinner party.

Some of the recipes have been adapted from dishes that were not originally intended to be used with baked potatoes, but with a little tweaking here and there they seem to get on well. Why not try one of your own, something you usually serve with rice or pasta for example?

All of the recipes in this book are suitable for vegetarians and vegans, so you can be sure that whoever you are cooking for will appreciate the wonders that this amazing vegetable has to offer.

Most of the ingredients used will be familiar to most people, but there are some that you may not have used before. There is a glossary at the end of the book that describes these ingredients but there are a few that deserve a mention here.

Tofu for example has had a bad press, often portrayed as some sort of dippy-hippy food, but if it is prepared properly it can add depths of texture and taste that will greatly enhance your culinary range.

Tofu, also known as beancurd, is made from raw soya beans and has been a staple food in many parts of the world for two thousand years, most notably China, where Western ailments like heart disease are very rare.

It's also important to use the right type of tofu. For the purposes of this book I have used only Firm Tofu, of the type that is sold by Cauldron Foods. I find that their organic firm tofu, which you can buy in most large supermarkets and in health food shops, is the most suited to Western tastes.

See the glossary at the end of the book for more information on this and other branded products used.

Tamari is made from fermented soya beans and adds flavour to foods without the drawbacks of the more commonly used salt. Shoyu is a very similar product to tamari and is used extensively in Japanese cooking.

Beans are good. We're all used to the humble tin of baked beans, but with less trouble than you might think, it's easy to buy dried beans of many different varieties and cook them yourself.

A note on cooking dried beans.

- First buy a packet of dried beans from a health food shop or supermarket.
- Tip them in a bowl and cover generously with water.
- Leave them soak overnight.
- Rinse them and boil them vigorously for ten minutes in fresh water.
- Simmer them until they go tender.
- Add them to recipes.
- Excess amounts can be frozen.

Some dried beans you can try.

Aduki Beans, Butter Beans, Chickpeas, Red Kidney Beans, Pinto Beans, Black-eye Beans, Haricot Beans (used for the common Baked Bean, also known as Navy Beans), Lima Beans and Fava Beans (or Broad Beans).

Finally, don't forget that cooking is an art as well as a skill; so don't be afraid to experiment, as long as you're prepared for the occasional disaster. It's a very rewarding experience to discover some new combination of flavours and textures.

However, be assured that all the recipes in this book are tried and tested.

Enjoy your baked potatoes.

Sabina Chance

POTATO HISTORY

Potato History

Potatoes are the world's number 1 vegetable.

Potatoes seem to be everywhere: they're in little plastic packets on the shelves of every food shop, on the menu in every restaurant and on the plates of everyone nearly every day, but they are relative newcomers to the diets of most of the world.

For many hundreds of years it was believed that the potato was a native plant of Virginia, but in fact the potato was introduced to Virginia, and many other places, probably during Francis Drake's voyage around the world in the late 1500s.

It is thought that wild potatoes were first used by the people of Peru 10,000 years ago, and that they were farmed and cultivated in the Andes, where it is too cold to grow maize, as long as 4,500 years ago.

The name potato is probably derived from the Indian name patata or papa.

The potato had a huge influence on early South American civilisations like the Incas who used representations of them in their art and developed religious ceremonies based on the vegetable. There are more than 1000 words used to describe potatoes and their associated products in the ancient Quechua language.

This humble, earthy vegetable was first brought to European attention by a Spanish conquistador when in 1537 he described finding maize, beans and a type of truffle, which we now know to be potato, after one of his raids on an Indian village.

For a few hundred years after its introduction to Europe the potato was viewed with suspicion, but it did eventually find its place as one of our favourite vegetables to the extent that dependence on it as a primary food source led to the consequences of the Irish Potato Famine of the 1800s.

The Irish had adopted the potato as their main food source because it yielded more food per acre of land than any other crop. For over two hundred years until 1845 the potato served Ireland well, to the extent that the potato became known as the Irish Potato all over the world to distinguish it from the sweet potato. Then the potato blight Phytophthora Infestans struck and potato crops were devastated, causing mass starvation and emigration.

Before the blight and of course afterwards, the Irish migrated all over the world and took the potato with them, introducing it to many countries and cultures, from where it spread further. Thus the potato has become the world's most eaten vegetable and continues to provide the basis for cheap, tasty and nutritious meals wherever it is used.

Sabina Chance

POTATO NUTRITION

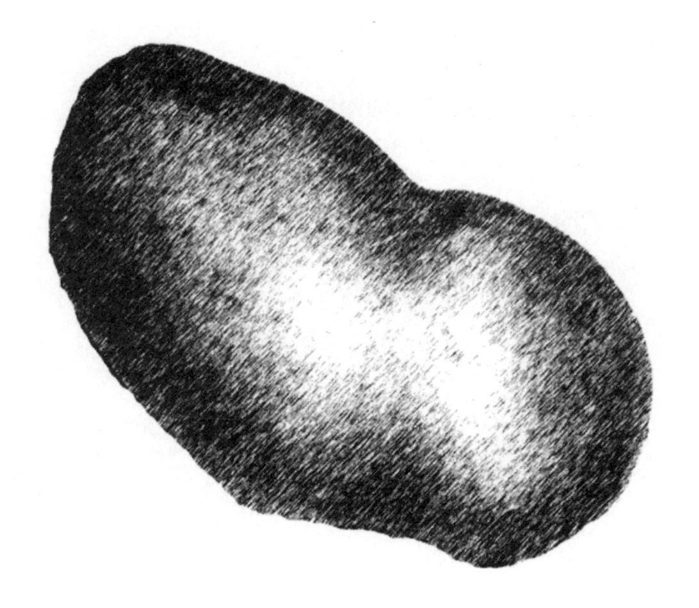

Potato Nutrition

Potatoes are now widely recognised as being very nutritious; they are a good source of complex carbohydrate, the type that the body needs for energy. They also contain many vitamins and minerals, when eaten with their skin on and provide a healthy, satisfying meal.

An average sized baking potato in its raw state provides the following basic nutrients.

Classic Potato per 100g

Energy	75 kcal
Protein	2 g
Carbohydrate	17 g
Fibre	2.2 g
Vitamin C	19 mg

In addition the potato contains these other vitamins and minerals, including 20% of the daily adult requirement for Potassium:

- Calcium
- Phosphorous
- Iron
- Sodium
- Potassium
- Magnesium
- Vitamin B1
- Vitamin B2
- Vitamin B3

"Eat the Skin"

The inhabitants of ancient South America, where the potato was first cultivated, used the potato along with maize as a staple food, and this undoubtedly helped them to worry less about day to day survival and concentrate more on building their culture and society.

The Incas used potatoes extensively in their diet. For example, potatoes were left in the open in the Andes so that they would dry out in the sun. They were then crushed into potato flour that could be stored for later use or carried on long journeys to provide sustenance.

Potatoes are good to eat and they are good for you. The vitamin C is a renowned antioxidant; it helps build a strong immune system and protects teeth and gums. Potatoes are low in sodium and a good source of potassium and therefore may help to protect against strokes and high blood pressure. In their unprepared state they also contain no fat.

Sabina Chance

TYPES OF POTATO

Types of Potato

Potato Varieties

Human beings have cultivated potatoes for thousands of years and along the way have developed many new varieties with differing characteristics. At the highest level, there are two main kinds of potatoes that we recognise – red and white, but behind these staples of the supermarket shelf there are, according to various sources, between 2000 and 5000 varieties of potatoes.

Most of these varieties are not in commercial production, so you are not going to see them on the shelves, in fact, the largest number of varieties ever seen in one place was at the Three Counties Potato Display as part of the Shropshire flower show in August 2004, where 589 varieties were collected together, including the variety known as Russian Banana.

Some other varieties listed on the European Cultivated Potato Database at http://www.europotato.org/ are Tiffany, Tosca and the Rural New Yorker.

According to the database there are 4,000 cultivars and 1,400 breeding lines of potato.

Much of the motivation in developing new strains of potato comes from the memory of the Irish Potato Famine.

Reliance on particular types of potato crop, which were devastated by Potato Blight, led to the death of many people and mass emigration from Ireland to America in the 1800s.

About 100 varieties are grown commercially in the UK, but three-quarters of all the potatoes we consume come from just 17 varieties.

The best types of potato for baking according to the British Potato Council Online Handbook at www.potato.org.uk, are:

- Admiral - New Variety
- Adora
- Avalanche
- Cara
- Cosmos - New Variety
- Estima
- Fianna
- Harmony - New Variety
- Remarka
- Riviera - New Variety
- Saxon
- Shannon
- Slaney
- Valor
- Verity - New Variety
- Xantia - New Variety
- Yukon Gold

Of these, the most recognisable types in the shops are Cara and Estima.

The Cara tubers are described as "Medium to large, short oval to round, parti-coloured red/white skin, cream flesh with medium eye depth."

According to other sources the best types of potato for baking are:

- Maris Piper
- King Edward
- Désirée
- Cara

or

- Marfona
- Kestrel
- Pomeroy
- Remarka
- Maris Piper

The lists go on . . . .

The more you look into it, the more likely you are to get confused. The best advice is to buy good quality potatoes that are the right size for your tastes, possibly sticking to those potatoes that are specifically labelled as Baking Potatoes, but don't be afraid to experiment.

Sabina Chance

HOW TO BAKE A POTATO

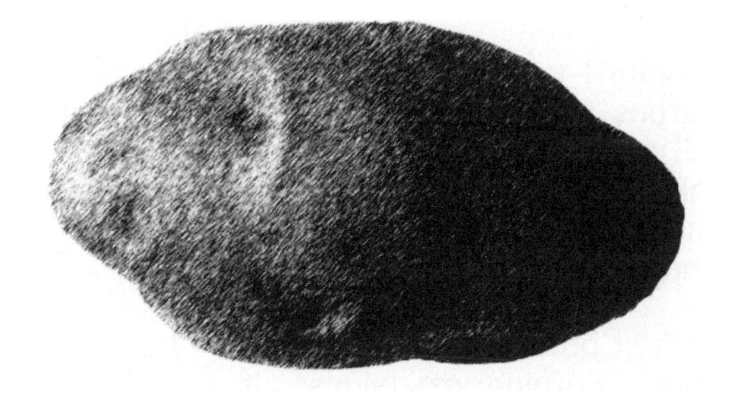

How to Bake a Potato

Baking a potato is simple isn't it? You just stick it in a hot oven and take it out when it's soft inside and not too burnt on the outside.

I have been cooking for my family and myself for half of my life and a bit more. I baked my first potato when I lived in a shared house in Cardiff.

Shameful I know, but up until then, with the over-generous financial assistance of my parents, I had lived mostly on expensive takeaways or restaurant meals with the odd tin of beans, heated and dumped on a slice of toast as my only contribution to the culinary arts.

That first potato was a revelation, I had approached it with a criminal casualness; just ran it under the tap and rubbed off the visible dirt, then rolled it haphazardly into the oven. I'd borrowed it off a housemate because I didn't have time to go to the takeaway – I was too busy getting ready for a night out and needed something to line my stomach in case I drank too much.

Luckily it turned out almost perfect, with a nice fluffy inside and a crisp but not tough skin. I smothered it in margarine and stuffed it with raw onion – it was amazing, something I alone had created from the raw materials of Mother Earth (except for the margarine) and it inspired me to develop my kitchen skills so that by the time I left that house to set up my own home, I was hooked, a cook for evermore.

My favourite method of baking a potato is:

Scrub it clean under a running tap.

Cut out the eyes and the scars it has acquired since its harvest.

Stab it a few times with a knife or a fork.

Hold it under the tap and run some more clean water over it to get rid of the excess starch created by cutting it.

Drizzle some sunflower oil over the potato.

Sprinkle a generous amount of sea salt over and rub it in, spreading the oil and the salt evenly over the potato.

Stick a metal skewer through the middle of the potato.

Put it in the centre of a hot oven, about 200 degrees C for an hour and twenty minutes.

Of course the oil drips onto the bottom of the oven, so I put a roasting tray on the shelf underneath for the first half hour to catch the drips.

Five minutes before the end of cooking, I take the potato from the oven, remove the skewer (careful, it's hot), wrap the potato in a clean tea towel and squeeze it gently until it gives.

Put the potato back in the oven and turn the heat on full for the last five or ten minutes.

Serve.

After talking to some of my friends and family, I discovered that there are many variations on this method, so I decided to conduct a survey. Listed below are some of the more sensible suggestions I received.

Keep it Simple
Josephine has a simple philosophy of the 'life's too short to stuff a mushroom' variety. This is her method.

Preheat the oven to almost maximum. After cleaning and rinsing the potato, stick a fork in several places. Put the potato on a high shelf in the oven and bake for almost an hour

Moisturise Your Skin
Misty likes to rub the potato lightly with olive oil before baking on a lower heat (180 degrees C) to make a softer skin.

Zap it
Caroline is a busy woman, with her two jobs and three children so sometimes she has to do everything she can to speed the process up. She

uses a microwave.

Pierce a medium to large potato all over with a fork. Put it in a microwave and cook on full power for up to 10 minutes (sometimes longer), turning over halfway to ensure even cooking.

Fluff it up
Owen's advice for fluffier potatoes is to pierce the potato with a fork; this lets the steam out and helps with the fluffiness. Before serving cut a cross in the top with a sharp knife and push the sides together to fluff it up.

Half-Baked
Gaynor is another busy woman, being both a head teacher and a karate expert, and likes to cut her potatoes in half lengthwise before placing them cut side down on an oiled baking tray, then baking for 35 minutes or more.

Sam's advice:
Ingredients for a successful baked potato.

- A nice big potato
- A good dollop of margarine
- A clean towel
- A fork and a microwave oven

Wash the potato and stab it several times with the fork. Heat on full power in the microwave for 4 minutes. Turn the potato over and heat on full power for another 4 minutes. Remove the potato and wrap it tight in the towel. Squeeze the potato through the towel until it gives.

Steam-Bake

Jerry wraps his in kitchen foil after washing them. He says "They're more like steamed potatoes than baked, because the potato cooks in its own steam as it can't escape, but they're just as nice in their own way, the skin is soft just as I like it."

Foil and onions

Frances is another aficionado of kitchen foil. She enjoys barbecues and loves to cut a potato in half lengthways. She then slices an onion and squashes it between the two halves of the potato along with a generous dollop of margarine.

She then wraps it in foil and puts it on the barbecue until it becomes succulent and soft and infused with the onion and margarine.

The professional touch

Ioan (Who is a professional chef by the way) bakes his potatoes 80% of the way without any additives; then he takes them out of the oven and cracks them with a rolling pin before drizzling lots of extra virgin olive oil and sprinkling them with caraway seeds. He then puts them back in the oven in a dish to finish the cooking

Massage it
Jessica rubs oil on hers, olive oil, then rubs fine sea salt and mixed herbs over them before cooking them for 1½ hours at 190 degrees C.

Other Variations
Baked potatoes are usually served whole, slit open and piled with the filling of your choice. You can also:

. Scoop the flesh out of the cooked potato
. Mash it in a bowl
. Mix in the filling
. Squeeze the mixture back into the potato skin
. Put it back in the oven for 10—20 minutes.

Hot Potatoes
Potatoes for the Barbecue should be wrapped in foil to avoid getting dirty.

My favourite method is to:

- Use medium size potatoes to shorten cooking time
- Wash the potatoes and remove any bad bits
- Cut a 1" / 2cm deep cross in the top of the potato with a sharp knife.
- Brush the potato lightly with sunflower oil and a little salt.
- Wrap the potato in two layers of cooking foil
- Place in the embers of a bonfire or on a barbecue
- Leave for 30 minutes initially
- Check now and again to see if it's cooked.

Sabina Chance

BEANS AND STUFF

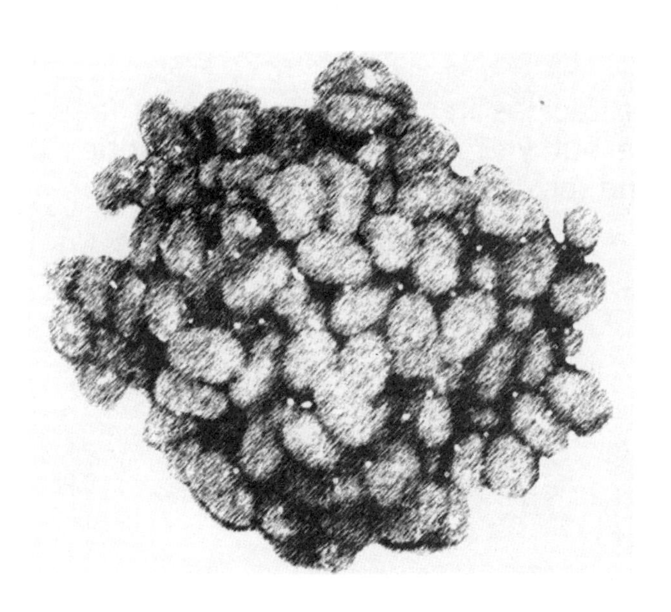

Beans and Stuff

The main focus of this section is the highly nutritious range of foods that include beans, pulses and tofu.

All the recipes in this section should feed 4 hungry people but you can adjust the quantities if you are cooking for more or for less.

Aduki Beans and Carrots

4 ozs / 115g Aduki beans – dry weight
1 or 2 tablespoons / 15ml – 30ml vegetable oil
1 large onion, chopped
2 cloves garlic, crushed
2 carrots, finely diced
3 tablespoons / 45ml tomato puree
2 teaspoons / 10ml mixed herbs
Salt and pepper to taste

Soak the Aduki beans overnight. Drain and rinse them. Bring to the boil in fresh water, continue to boil rapidly for 10 minutes, reduce the heat, cover and simmer until soft (about 45 minutes). Keep the beans and the cooking water.

Heat a tablespoon of oil in a wok or a large frying pan. Fry the onions and garlic for five minutes, add the carrots and sauté until the carrots begin to soften. Add beans and their cooking liquid, herbs, salt and pepper and tomato puree. Add extra water if necessary and simmer for a further 30 – 40 minutes.

Notes:
Aduki (or Adzuki) Beans are small red beans originating from China. They are extremely savoury and have a high iron content.

Black Eye Stew

8 ozs / 225g black eye beans – dry weight
1 or 2 tablespoons / 15ml – 30ml vegetable oil
1 large onion, chopped
2 cloves garlic, crushed
3 ozs / 85g green beans, washed and cut into 1" / 2cm lengths
1 small red or green pepper chopped
1 x 14oz / 400g can chopped tomatoes
2 tablespoons / 30ml tomato puree
2 tablespoons / 30ml dried parsley (or a handful of finely chopped fresh flat parsley)
Salt and pepper to taste
Pinch chilli powder

Soak the black eye beans overnight. Drain and rinse them. Bring to the boil in fresh water, continue to boil rapidly for 10 minutes, reduce the heat, cover and simmer until soft (about 20 minutes). Keep the beans and the cooking water.

Heat a tablespoon of oil in a wok or a large frying pan. Fry the onions and garlic, add green beans and pepper – sauté until the green beans begin to soften.

Add black eye beans and their cooking liquid, tomatoes, tomato puree, parsley, salt and pepper and chilli. Simmer for a further 20 - 30 minutes.

Potato Bolognese #1

¾ pint / 425ml boiling water
3½ ozs / 100g dried TVP Mince
½ oz / 15g soya margarine
1 onion chopped
1 parsnip finely chopped
1 carrot finely chopped
1 stick celery finely chopped
salt and pepper to taste
1 tablespoon / 15ml sugar
1 bay leaf
2 tablespoons / 30ml tamari or shoyu
1 x 14oz / 400g tin chopped tomatoes

Pour the boiling water over the TVP in a bowl. Melt the margarine in a saucepan and sauté the onion, parsnip, carrot and celery for 5 - 10 minutes. Add the now-hydrated TVP, salt, pepper, sugar, bay leaf, tamari and tomatoes to the pan and simmer for 15 - 20 minutes.

Potato Bolognese #2
Another Variation

1 tablespoon / 15ml olive oil
1 onion, chopped
2 cloves garlic, crushed
½ green pepper, chopped
4 ozs / 115g button mushrooms, chopped
2 medium carrots, diced
3 ozs/ 85g dried TVP mince, re-hydrated
1 x 14oz / 400g tin chopped tomatoes
3 tablespoons / 45ml tomato puree
Salt and pepper to taste

Sauté the onions, garlic, pepper, mushrooms and carrots in the oil in a covered pan until the juices permeate and the carrots start to soften. Add the rest of the ingredients and cook for twenty minutes.

Cauliflower Tofu
(Cauli Sans Cheese)

1 medium cauliflower, cleaned and left whole
1 large onion, chopped
2 cloves garlic, crushed
4 tablespoons / 60ml vegetable oil
3 heaped tablespoons / 50ml plain white flour
1 vegetable stock cube, dissolved in the cooking water from the cauliflower, or plain water
1 teaspoon / 5ml yeast extract
Salt and pepper to taste
Boiling water if necessary
6 ozs / 175g tofu, mashed

Cook the cauliflower in a large pan half covered with water. Meanwhile fry the onion and garlic for a few minutes in the vegetable oil, until they are soft but not brown. Add the flour and continue stirring and cooking for a minute or two until the oil and flour form a paste. Add the water from the cauliflower (with the dissolved stock cube) and the yeast extract, salt and pepper. Continue adding boiling water if necessary, stirring all the time until a rich thick sauce is formed. Mash the tofu and add it to the sauce. Warm up again. Remove the cauliflower from the pan carefully and put it in a deep round serving dish. Pour the sauce over it.

Best Chilli Ever
(compliments of Ceri)

2 – 3 tablespoons / 30ml – 45ml of sunflower oil
2 – 3 medium onions, chopped
6 – 8 cloves of garlic, crushed
3 – 8 finger chillies (depending on taste), chopped finely
2 green chillies, chopped finely
2½ medium carrots, cut into small cubes
1 green pepper, cut into small pieces
½ red pepper, cut into small pieces
4 or 5 mushrooms, cut into small pieces
1½ x 14oz / 400g tins of chopped tomatoes
3½ fl oz / 100ml tomato puree
1 x 14oz / 400g tin red kidney beans
1 x 7oz / 200g small tin sweetcorn kernels
1 heaped teaspoon / 5ml – 8ml salt (or to taste)
1 teaspoon / 5ml sugar, Demerara if possible
freshly ground black pepper to taste

Fry the onions and garlic in the oil, stirring constantly for 2 or 3 minutes. Add the chillies and fry for another 2 or 3 minutes.

Add the carrots and peppers and fry for another 1 or 2 minutes.

Add the mushrooms, continue to stir fry until the onion starts turning brown.

Add the tomatoes and tomato puree, kidney beans and sweetcorn. Then add the salt and sugar.

Mix it all together and add a little extra water if necessary.

Bring to the boil for a few minutes then reduce the heat and simmer on a moderate heat with the lid on for 30 minutes, checking now and again for sticking.

Before serving sprinkle with freshly ground black pepper

Note: Remove the seeds from the chillies if you're not used to them to make them less hot

Chilli not Chilly

3 ozs / 85g dry weight TVP mince, re-hydrated
2 tablespoons / 30ml vegetable oil
1 onion chopped
2 cloves garlic crushed
2 carrots diced
1 fresh green chilli chopped
1 green pepper chopped
2 tablespoons / 30ml tomato puree
1 x 14oz / 400g tin of red kidney beans
salt to taste
1 oz / 25g walnut pieces
Fresh parsley – if available

If you are using dried Red Kidney beans: soak them overnight in plenty of boiling water, rinse well, boil rapidly for at least 10 minutes (this is **essential** to remove possible toxins), reduce heat, cover and simmer until the beans are well cooked.

Place the dried TVP in a bowl and cover generously with boiling water, leave to soak. Pour vegetable oil into a wok or a deep frying pan.

Add the onions, garlic, carrots, and chilli. (If you are using chilli powder instead of fresh chilli add it later with the tomato puree.)

Sauté, until the onions are soft then add the green pepper. Continue stir-frying until the carrots are almost soft.

Add tomato puree, TVP, Red Kidney beans and salt. Add extra water if necessary.

Bring the chilli to boiling point - mixing occasionally to prevent sticking - and simmer for a few minutes. Garnish with walnuts and fresh parsley if available.

Notes:

The walnuts provide a delicious crunchy bite; omit them if you don't like them. If you object to TVP use more carrots or beans instead.

Cannelloni Bean and Vegetable Casserole

(inspired by Andrew)

1 onion, sliced
1 leek, washed and sliced into thin rounds
1" / 2cm piece root ginger, sliced thinly
1 small chilli, deseeded and chopped
3 tablespoons / 45ml sunflower oil
2 teaspoons / 10ml of dried mixed herbs
2oz / 55g pine nut kernels
1 small swede, cut in ½" / 1cm cubes
2 large carrots, diced
2 sticks celery, chopped into 1" / 2cm pieces
8ozs / 225g green beans cut into 1" / 2cm lengths
1 x 14oz / 400 g tin Cannelloni Beans
2 tablespoons / 30ml tomato puree
salt and freshly ground black pepper to taste
a few dashes of tamari or shoyu

Mix all the ingredients in a large casserole dish, cover and cook in a hot oven - 225 degrees centigrade for 45 minutes.

Check to see if the vegetables are cooked, mix well, add a little water and cook for a further 20 minutes if necessary.

Green-Legged Tofu

8 ozs / 225g green beans, cut into finger length strips
8 ozs / 225g mange tout, trimmed
Large onion, sliced
5 cloves garlic, crushed
2 tablespoons / 30ml vegetable oil
9ozs / 250g firm tofu, cubed and marinated in tamari (soy sauce) for 30 minutes
Salt and pepper to taste

Steam the green beans and mange tout until just beginning to get tender. Meanwhile fry the onion and garlic in the vegetable oil for a few minutes. Add the marinated tofu and fry until it starts to go golden brown. Add the beans and mange tout and mix well on high heat. Sprinkle with salt and pepper and serve.

Continental Lentil Mousakka

You can substitute other types of lentils such as green lentils or brown lentils. It is best to choose an unpolished whole lentil rather than the split red lentil as these tend to go too mushy.

6 ozs / 175g continental lentils dry weight, soaked overnight and cooked for 30 – 40 minutes
1 large aubergine, sliced into rounds
salt
olive oil for frying the aubergine
1 large onion, chopped
3 cloves garlic, crushed
2 tablespoons / 30ml olive oil
4 ozs / 115g mushrooms, sliced
2 celery sticks, chopped
1 x 14oz / 400g can of chopped tomatoes
6 tablespoons / 90ml tomato puree
quarter pint /150ml of Soya milk
2 tablespoons / 30ml vegan Parmesan cheese (Parmazano)
salt and pepper to taste

Arranged the sliced aubergine in layers coating each layer liberally with salt, let stand for half an hour.

Sauté the onions and garlic for a few minutes in the olive oil. Add the mushrooms and celery and sauté some more until the celery is cooked.

Add the tomatoes, tomato puree, drained cooked lentils and seasoning and cook gently for ten minutes.

Rinse the aubergines well to remove the salt and bitter juices, and fry the slices in olive oil until browned on both sides.

Layer the aubergine and the lentil mixture in a casserole dish finishing off with a layer of aubergine slices.

Pour the soya milk over the top and sprinkle with the Parmazano (you may be able to substitute something like nutritional yeast).

Prick the top of the mixture with a fork so that some of the soya milk soaks in.

Bake in a medium oven for 20 - 30 minutes.

Roasted Med Veg and Red

2 red onions, sliced roughly
2 cloves garlic crushed
1 red pepper, sliced
2 courgettes, sliced
4 ozs / 115g pitted black olives
4 ozs / 115g button mushrooms, washed and halved
1 medium aubergine, cut in chunks
1 x 14oz / 400g tin red kidney beans
6 tomatoes quartered
3 tablespoons / 45ml of olive oil
Salt and pepper to taste

Put everything in a deep oven tray. Drizzle with the olive oil, season and roast under a hot grill for 45 minutes, turning occasionally until it's all nicely roasted.

Bean Medley * FAT FREE *

1 large carrot cut into small cubes
8 ozs / 225g green beans, cut into 1" / 2cm pieces
1 x 7oz / 200g small tin of sweetcorn kernels
1 x 7oz / 200g small tin of borlotti or pinto Beans
1 x 14oz / 400g tin of chick peas
1 onion chopped and sliced
2 cloves garlic, crushed
1 small chilli, deseeded and chopped finely
Juice of 1 lemon
1 teaspoon / 5ml sugar
1 x 14 oz / 400g tin of chopped tomatoes
Salt and pepper to taste

Steam cook the carrots and green beans - do not overcook.

Meanwhile put all the other ingredients into a saucepan, bring to the boil and simmer for a few minutes. Add the cooked carrots and green beans and bring back to the boil. Cover and simmer for 30 minutes, leave the lid off to reduce the liquid towards the end of the cooking time.

Mushroom Yoganoff

2 tablespoons / 30ml cooking oil
1 large onion – sliced
3 cloves garlic – crushed
1 large carrot – sliced thinly
8 ozs / 225g button mushrooms – halved
3 ozs / 85g continental lentils (dry weight) – cooked as for the Lentil Mousakka on page 44
1 x 14oz / 400g tin of tomatoes
1 tablespoon / 15ml tomato puree
5 fluid ounces / 150 ml water or cooking liquid from the lentils
1 teaspoon / 5ml dried oregano
Salt and pepper to taste
Small carton vegan yoghurt or 1/2 pint / 300ml soya milk

Heat the oil in a wok and add the onions and garlic – cook for a minute or two. Add the carrots and sauté on a high heat for a few minutes. Add the mushrooms and sauté for a few more minutes. Add the cooked lentils, tomatoes, tomato puree, lentil juice or water, oregano, salt and pepper. Bring to the boil and simmer until the carrots are soft. Just before serving stir in the yoghurt and heat through.

Chilled Chilli Bean Salsa

2 x 14oz / 400g cans red kidney beans drained or 1½lb / 700g of soaked and cooked beans; partially mashed
1 red onion chopped
5 or 6 chopped tomatoes or 1 x 14oz / 400g tin of chopped tomatoes
3 cloves garlic crushed
1 or 2 red chillies finely chopped
salt and pepper to taste
½ teaspoon / 2.5ml ground cumin
a handful of fresh coriander or parsley

Mash or blend all the ingredients except the coriander or parsley until a nice chunky paste forms. Mix in the coriander or parsley. Leave to chill in a refrigerator before serving. You can also heat the Salsa up and cook it gently for 10 minutes, if you prefer a hot filling.

Rustic Tofu & Courgette

2 or 3 tablespoons / 30ml – 45ml vegetable oil
2 onions, sliced roughly
2 cloves of garlic, crushed casually
2 courgettes sliced haphazardly
9 oz / 250g block of firm tofu, chopped into irregular cubes
1 x 14oz / 400g tin chopped tomatoes
3 tablespoons / 45ml of tomato puree
Extra water if needed
1 teaspoon / 5ml dried oregano
Salt and crushed black pepper to taste

Fry the onion and garlic in a wok with the oil until just starting to brown. Add the courgettes. Stir-fry for 5 - 10 minutes. Add the tofu and continue stir-frying for a few more minutes. Add the tomatoes, tomato puree, herbs and spices to taste. Stir well, bring to the boil and simmer for 15 minutes, adding extra water if it gets too sticky.

Scrambled Tofu, Mushrooms and Leeks

2ozs / 55g vegan margarine
2 onions chopped
2 cloves garlic crushed
1 large leek, washed and sliced
4 ozs / 115g button mushrooms, washed and sliced
2 x 9 oz / 250g blocks firm tofu, mashed
2 teaspoons / 10ml ground turmeric
1 teaspoon / 5ml salt

Fry the onions, garlic, leeks and mushrooms in the margarine until the leeks are soft. Add the tofu, turmeric and salt. Leave on the heat and mix well until the tofu is warmed and the turmeric colour is consistent.

Taco Style Taters
(Compliments of Laura)

Filling:
1 onion, chopped
2 cloves garlic, minced
2 – 3 tablespoons / 30 – 45ml sunflower oil
1 red or yellow pepper, chopped
1 - 2 fresh green chillies, chopped finely
1 teaspoon / 5ml ground cumin
2 teaspoons / 10ml ground coriander
1½ - 2 x 14oz / 400g cans refried beans
(or soaked, cooked and mashed pinto beans)
salt and ground black pepper to taste

Guacamole:
2 ripe avocadoes, use the flesh scooped out
½ an onion, finely chopped
1 small green chilli, finely chopped
2 - 3 tablespoons / 30ml – 45ml fresh coriander, finely chopped
1 or 2 tablespoons/ 15ml – 30ml of lemon juice

1 x whole lettuce shredded (iceberg)
Few pickled jalapenos (optional)

Fry the onion and garlic in the oil until the onion starts to soften. Add the peppers and continue frying for about 5 minutes. Add chilli, cumin and coriander and stir in well. Lower heat and add refried beans, mixing in well until heated through.

Season to taste.

To make the guacamole, mash the avocado flesh with a fork until it is smooth. Mix in the onion, chilli, fresh coriander and lemon juice to taste.

Spoon the refried beans into the potatoes. Top with a generous dollop of creamy guacamole, top with shredded lettuce and if liked, pickled jalapenos (These are available in jars from most groceries). You may also like to add salsa, Cheezly or Plamil egg free Mayonnaise.

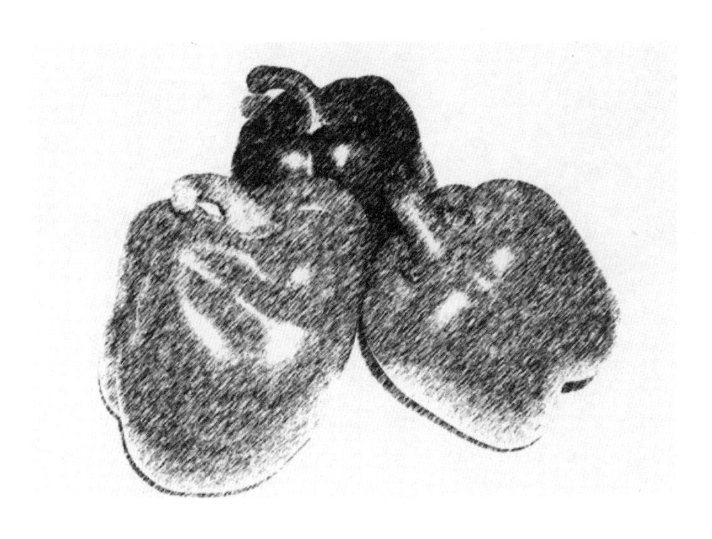

Spicy Mexican Filling

2 tablespoons/ 30ml vegetable oil
2 onions, chopped
4 cloves garlic crushed
1 large courgette, cut into thin strips
4 ozs / 115g button mushrooms, sliced
1 large carrot, cut into matchsticks
2 small tins of Discovery refried beans
2 x 14oz / 400g tin chopped tomatoes
6 tablespoons / 90ml tomato puree

Sauté the onions, garlic, courgette, mushrooms and carrots in the oil in a covered pan until the juices permeate and the carrots start to soften. Add the rest of the ingredients and cook gently for twenty minutes.

Tofu, Leek and Mushroom Bake

1 medium leek, washed and sliced finely
6 ozs / 175g of mushrooms, sliced
2 tablespoons / 30ml of sunflower oil
9 oz / 250g block of firm tofu
7 fl ozs / 200ml soya milk
1 clove garlic, minced
Large pinch black pepper
Juice of ½ a lemon
½ teaspoon / 2.5ml salt
1 teaspoon / 5ml dried marjoram
2 teaspoons / 10ml paprika
Margarine for greasing

Sauté the leeks and mushrooms in the sunflower oil until the leeks are soft. Meanwhile break the tofu up roughly and put it in a blender with the soya milk, garlic, black pepper, lemon juice, salt, and marjoram. Put the cooked leek and mushroom mixture in the bottom of a greased casserole dish and pour the blended tofu mixture onto it. Stir gently, sprinkle with paprika, and cook uncovered in a hot oven for 15 - 20 minutes.

Tofu, Mushrooms and Olives

2 x 9 oz / 250g blocks firm tofu, cut into ½" / 1cm cubes
2 large onions, sliced
4 cloves garlic, crushed
1lb / 450g button mushrooms washed and halved
8 ozs, 225g pitted black olives
few dashes tamari, shoyu or other soy sauce
salt and pepper
generous slurp of olive oil

Put everything in a casserole dish. Mix well. Put a lid on it and bake in a hot oven for 30 minutes, allowing the juices to permeate and the tofu to go crisp around the edges.

Saucy Tofu Turmeric

2 tablespoons / 30ml margarine for frying
2 x 9oz / 250g blocks of firm tofu cut into small chunks
2 teaspoons / 10ml turmeric
2 tablespoons / 30ml tamari
2 tablespoons / 30ml tomato puree
¾ pint / 425ml water

Melt the margarine in a frying pan. Fry the tofu on medium heat for 5 - 10 minutes, stirring to avoid sticking until browned and chewy. Add the turmeric and stir in. Add the tamari and stir, add the tomato puree and mix well. Add the water and bring to the boil. Turn the heat down and simmer gently until the sauce thickens. Nice with a green vegetable.

Ratatouille Americano

2 – 3 tablespoonfuls / 30ml – 45ml olive oil
2 onions chopped
1 large aubergine, cut into 1" / 2cm cubes
1 large courgette diced
1 large red pepper, cut into 1" / 2cm square chunks
5 cloves garlic crushed
1lb / 450g fresh tomatoes chopped, or 1 x 14oz / 400g tin chopped tomatoes
6 teaspoons / 90ml tomato puree
1 teaspoon dried rosemary
Salt and pepper to taste

Sauté the onions, aubergine, courgette, pepper and the garlic in the olive oil, in an open pan on a high heat, stirring constantly to avoid sticking, for five minutes. Reduce the heat to minimum, put a lid on the pan and let cook for ten to fifteen minutes, checking now and again for sticking. Add the tomatoes, tomato puree, rosemary, salt and pepper and a little extra water if necessary. Bring to the boil and simmer in a covered pan for 15 to 20 minutes.

Tahini sauce and red salad

Medium red cabbage, raw or steamed lightly, cooled and chopped
3 red onions sliced finely
1½ lbs / 675g cooked beetroot cut into small cubes
6 tablespoons / 90ml cider vinegar
12oz / 300ml tahini
½ teaspoon / 2.5ml salt
1 teaspoon / 5ml paprika

Mix all the ingredients in a large bowl.

Falafels with Tahini sauce

½ pound / 225g of dried chickpeas
1 onion, chopped finely
1 clove garlic, crushed
½oz / 15g of fresh coriander or parsley leaves chopped finely
1 teaspoon / 5ml ground coriander
1 teaspoon / 5ml ground cumin
1 teaspoon / 5ml salt
Vegetable oil for deep frying

Soak the chickpeas for at least 8 hours in plenty of cold water, rinse them in running water. Grind the chickpeas in a food processor or with a hand mincer to a paste. Add the other ingredients and mix well. Form the mixture into slightly flattened balls (a dessertspoon is useful for this) Drop the falafels a few at a time into very hot oil and cook until golden brown.

For the sauce:
6ozs / 175g tahini
2 tablespoons / 30ml tamari or shoyu soya sauce
3 tablespoons / 45ml water
7 or 8 spring onions chopped into small pieces

Mix all the ingredients with a hand whisk or a fork – pour over the falafels and serve.

Red Bean and Sweetcorn Salsa

2 x 14oz, 400g cans red kidney beans, drained and mashed roughly
1 x 7oz / 200g tin of sweetcorn kernels
1 x 14oz / 400g tin chopped tomatoes or 5 or 6 chopped fresh tomatoes
half a handful of chopped parsley or coriander
1 red pepper, chopped into small pieces (roast beforehand for a less crunchy texture)
Juice of 1 lime
3 green chillies chopped finely
1 teaspoon / 5ml ground cumin
Salt and pepper to taste

Mix all the ingredients well. Best chilled, but you can heat it up and cook it gently for 10 minutes if you fancy a hot dinner.

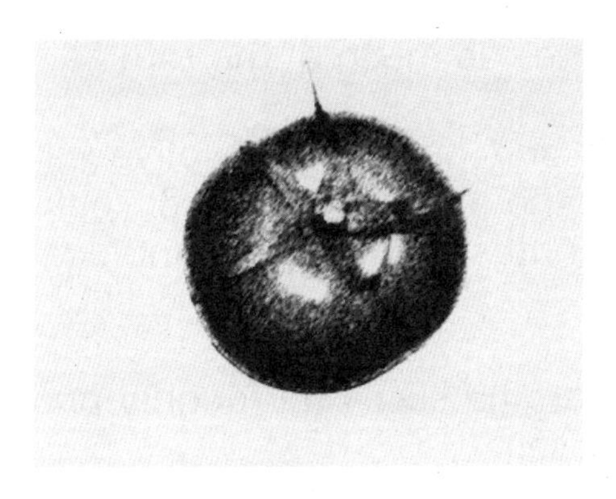

Sautéed Aubergine, Tofu and Tomatoes

1 medium aubergine, sliced thinly
plenty of sea salt
1 x 9oz / 250g block of tofu, cut into ¼" / 5mm thick rectangles of 1" x 1" / 2cm x 2cm
3 tablespoons / 45ml of tamari
1 onion, sliced thinly
1 or 2 cloves garlic, crushed
3 tablespoons / 45ml of extra virgin olive oil
6 ozs / 150g button mushrooms, sliced thinly
1lb / 450g fresh tomatoes, sliced

Layer the aubergine slices on a plate, liberally sprinkling each layer with sea salt. Let stand for 30 minutes.

Place the tofu rectangles on a plate and sprinkle generously with the tamari, making sure that every piece is covered. Let stand while preparing the rest of the dish, turning occasionally to make sure the tamari permeates as much of the tofu as possible.

Fry the onion and garlic in the olive oil for a few minutes, add the mushrooms and cook on a low heat for 10 minutes, stirring now and again to avoid sticking.

Rinse the aubergine slices thoroughly under the tap to remove the salt.

Add the aubergine to the pan and cook on a low heat for another five minutes. Add the tofu, including any excess tamari and cook for another 10 minutes, stirring to avoid sticking.

Finally add the tomatoes, cover the pan and cook on a low heat for 20 minutes.

Sabina Chance

CURRIES

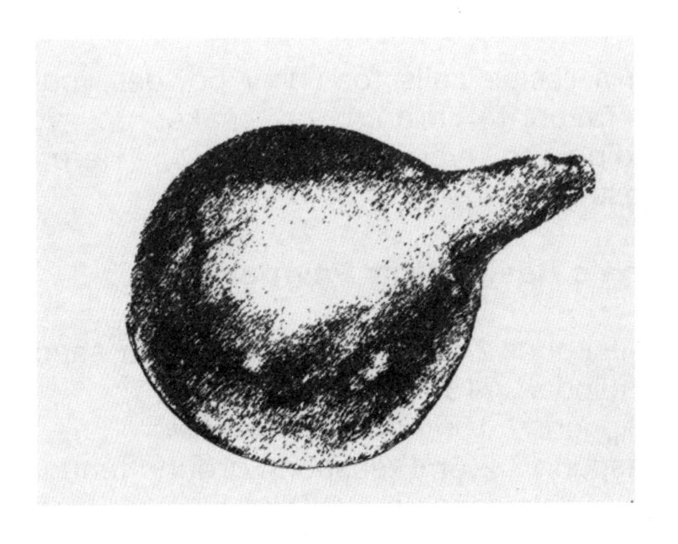

Curries

Curries are always ready to give a little extra zing to a meal. If prepared carefully and with the right combination of spices, they can be extremely tasty without being too 'hot'.

Sometimes a shop-bought packet of 'curry powder' will suffice, although the contents of the packets are sometimes a bit hit-and-miss.

When a recipe calls for curry powder you can use your favourite brand, or make up your own according to your own tastes. Here is one suggestion:

Sabina's Basic Curry Powder

2 tablespoons / 30ml ground coriander seeds
1 tablespoon / 15ml ground cumin
2 teaspoons / 10ml ground turmeric
½ teaspoon / 2.5ml teaspoon ground fenugreek seeds (whole seeds are OK)
½ teaspoon / 2.5ml ground cloves
½ teaspoon / 2.5ml chilli powder
½ teaspoon / 2.5ml ground ginger

Carrot and Chick Pea Curry - Balti Style

3 tablespoons / 45ml vegetable ghee or oil
2 onions, sliced thickly
3 medium carrots, sliced thinly
4 cloves garlic, crushed
1 small green pepper. chopped
4oz / 115g button mushrooms, sliced thinly
3 or 4 tablespoons / 45ml – 60ml curry powder
1 x 14oz / 400g can of cooked chick peas
6 tablespoons, 90ml tomato puree
Juice of half a lemon
Dash of soya milk
Salt to taste

Heat the oil in a wok or saucepan. Fry the onions in the ghee/oil for a few minutes. Let them go a little brown but not burnt. Add the rest of the prepared vegetables and sauté, stirring to stop sticking, until the carrots have started to go tender. Add the curry powder and stir-fry for a minute or so, until the aroma of the spices is released. Add the chickpeas (including the liquid from the can), tomato puree, lemon juice, soya milk and salt. Bring to the boil, then simmer for 15 - 20 minutes.

*NOTE: As with all these recipes, canned chickpeas and beans are for convenience only. Alternatively, you could soak and cook them and freeze the excess.

Aubergine and Spinach Curry

1 large aubergine, cut into ½" / 1cm cubes
salt
3 tablespoons / 45ml ghee or vegetable oil
1 teaspoon / 5ml caraway seeds
1 large onion, sliced
4 cloves garlic, crushed
1 fresh chilli, chopped finely
1" / 2cm piece of fresh ginger, peeled and grated
1 lb / 450g spinach, washed
1 x 14oz / 400g tin of chopped tomatoes
2 tablespoons / 30ml ground coriander
1 tablespoon / 15ml ground cumin
2 teaspoons /10ml ground turmeric
1 teaspoon / 5ml salt
Juice of half a lemon

Place the aubergine in a bowl and sprinkle generously with salt. Cover and leave to stand while preparing the rest of the ingredients or for about 30 minutes.

Heat the ghee or oil in a heavy pan. Place the seeds in the hot oil and when they begin to pop add the onion, garlic, chilli, and ginger. Fry until the onion is soft and turning brown.

Rinse the aubergine and add to the pan. Stir fry for 5 - 10 minutes until the aubergine starts to go soft and is well coated with the other ingredients. Stir in the spinach, mix well and cook for another 2 or 3 minutes.

Add the tomatoes, coriander, turmeric, and ground cumin. Add a little salt at this stage if desired. If the mixture is a little dry add some water.

Cook on a moderate heat until the aubergines are cooked through. Add the lemon juice and more water if needed. Add the water a little at a time because this mixture should be moist but not runny.

Mix thoroughly and leave to stand on a low heat for a few minutes before serving.

Red Lentil Masala

1 medium onion chopped
2 tablespoons / 30ml cooking oil
2 large carrots, diced finely
½lb / 225g red lentils, washed thoroughly
2 tablespoons / 30ml curry powder
Salt to taste
2 pints / 1.2 litres water
3 tablespoons / 45ml tomato puree
1 lemon

Fry the onion in the oil until well cooked. Add the chopped carrot and the lentils to the onion and sauté for a few minutes, stirring all the time to stop the lentils sticking or burning. Add the curry powder and salt and stir in. Add the water and tomato puree and stir well. Bring to the boil, cover and simmer 30 - 40 minutes adding more water if necessary, until it's thick and creamy.

Serve hot with a slice of lemon.

Curried Chickpeas

2 onions, chopped
2 cloves garlic, crushed
4 tablespoons / 60ml vegetable oil or ghee
4 tablespoons / 60ml curry powder or:
    2 tablespoons / 30ml ground coriander
    2 teaspoons / 10ml ground turmeric
    1 teaspoon / 5ml mild chilli powder
    1 teaspoon / 5ml ground ginger
    1 teaspoon / 5ml salt
2 x 14oz / 400g tins of chickpeas
2 x 14 oz / 400g tins chopped tomatoes
6 tablespoons / 90ml tomato puree

Fry the onion and garlic in the ghee until the onions start to go brown but not burnt. Add the curry powder and stir it in for a minute. Add the chickpeas, tomatoes and tomato puree. Bring to the boil and cook for 15 minutes. Add more salt if necessary.

Simple Curry * FAT FREE *

2 onions, chopped
2 x 14oz / 400g cans of chopped tomatoes
4 cloves garlic, crushed
4 tablespoons / 60ml curry powder
2 carrots, diced and steam cooked
8ozs / 225g frozen green peas
small cauliflower, cut into florets and steamed

Cook the onions and garlic in the tomatoes until the onions are soft. Add more water if it begins to dry up too much. Add the curry powder and cook for a further five minutes. Finally add the carrots, peas and cauliflower, bring to the boil and simmer for five minutes for the flavours to blend.

Quick Curry

FOR THE SAUCE:

1 onion, chopped
2 cloves garlic, crushed
4 tablespoons / 60ml vegetable ghee or oil
4 tablespoons / 60ml curry powder
1 pint / 600ml boiling water or vegetable stock
6 tablespoons / 90ml tomato puree
1 level teaspoon salt

OTHER INGREDIENTS:

2 lb / 900g steam-cooked vegetables in season or frozen vegetables, e.g: carrots, peas, mushrooms, cauliflower, broccoli, baby sweetcorn.

To make the sauce: sauté the onion and garlic in the oil or ghee until browned and soft. Add the curry powder and cook for 2 minutes stirring to avoid burning. Add the stock or water, tomato puree and salt and bring to the boil, then simmer for 10 – 15 minutes.

Add the cooked vegetables, heat up and cook for another 5 minutes.

Mushroom Bhaji Light * FAT FREE *

1lb / 450g mushrooms, sliced
1" / 2cm piece ginger crushed
2 teaspoons / 10ml yellow mustard seeds
salt to taste
2 teaspoons / 10ml turmeric
2 x 14oz / 400g tins of chopped tomatoes

Dry roast the mushrooms in a wok or wide frying pan, stirring until they start to cook. Add the spices and stir-fry for a minute. Add the tomatoes, bring to the boil and simmer until the excess liquid has evaporated.

Spicy Chick Peas and Carrots

2 tablespoons / 30ml vegetable oil
2 large carrots, diced
2 red onions, chopped
10 spring onions, cleaned and chopped finely
8 cloves garlic, crushed
4 tablespoons / 60ml curry powder
2 x 14oz / 400g cans chickpeas un-drained
4 tablespoons / 60ml tomato puree

Heat the oil in a pan, add the carrots, onions, spring onions and garlic. Cover the pan and sauté, stirring to avoid sticking, until the carrots are beginning to soften. Turn the heat up, add the curry powder and stir in, cooking and stirring for a minute or so. Add the chickpeas and the tomato puree; stir well and simmer for 20 minutes.

TVP Chunk Curry

This is a very 'Meaty' curry.

8 ozs / 225g of dried TVP Chunks
2 onions sliced thinly
3 cloves garlic, crushed
2 large carrots, diced
3 tablespoons / 45ml sunflower oil
3 tablespoons / 45ml curry powder
4 tablespoons / 60ml tomato puree
2 teaspoons / 10ml Garam Masala

Cover the TVP in boiling water and soak for half an hour. Fry the onions, garlic and carrots in the oil until the carrots are beginning to soften. Stir in the curry powder and cook for a minute, add the soaked TVP along with the excess liquid and the tomato puree. Stir and cook on a moderate heat for 15 minutes until a thick sauce is formed.

Sprinkle the Garam Masala on just before serving and stir in gently.

Sabina Chance

STIR FRIES

Stir Fries

Stir-fries are as varied as the people that make them. There are some basics that you should know, but this is a very forgiving method of cooking so don't be afraid to experiment when you've grasped the essentials.

Only your imagination limits the results that you can achieve when you prepare a stir-fry. Most vegetables are suitable for stir-frying and you can add other ingredients to give your creation that extra bit of pizzazz.

ESSENTIALS

Onion, Garlic, Shoyu or Tamari, Vegetable Oil *.

* You can also experiment with other types of oil such as those with strong tastes like walnut oil and sesame oil, or oils infused with garlic and other spices.

BASIC VEGETABLES

Choose from the vegetables that you have to hand; some suggestions: Carrots, Sweet Potatoes, Peppers, Courgettes, Aubergine, Parsnips, Turnip, Swede, Celery, Shredded Cabbage, Bamboo Shoots, Water Chestnuts, Mange Tout, Runner Beans, Mushrooms, Beansprouts, Cauliflower, Broccoli, Leeks, Baby Sweetcorn, Shallots.

EXTRA INGREDIENTS

Choose from a wide range of extra ingredients, some suggestions: cooked Chick Peas, Kidney Beans, Sunflower Seeds, Pumpkin Seeds, Sesame Seeds, Firm Tofu, Seitan, TVP, Herbs & Spices according to taste.

Choose a selection of items from the above lists or make up your own.

Slice or chop the onions, crush the garlic, add to the vegetable oil in a wok and stir-fry for a few minutes. Turn the heat down on the wok and prepare the vegetables. There are two main methods of preparing the vegetables:

1. Choose the vegetables that have the longest cooking time first and work your way down to the ones with the shortest cooking time, preparing each vegetable and adding it to the wok as you go along.

or

2: Prepare all the vegetables first and add them all at once to the wok.

Each ingredient will require a different technique in its preparation; for example Carrots are best cut into thin strips, Courgettes may be sliced into disks of about ¼" / 5mm thick or cut into strips, Broccoli and Cauliflower should be separated into flowers, Baby Sweetcorn and Mange Tout can be added whole after washing and trimming.

Whichever method you choose, stir the ingredients continually to prevent sticking and to distribute the heat. Add the Shoyu as you go being careful not too overdo it. Add the extra ingredients when the vegetables are almost cooked. Towards the end of cooking, put a lid on the wok and turn the heat down to a minimum.

Left over stir-fry can be turned into a curry very easily: Heat the stir-fry up and add tomato puree or tinned tomatoes and curry powder, stir well over the heat and add boiling water or vegetable stock, simmer and stir until the right consistency is reached.

Here are some specific recipes for stir-fries, but don't be afraid to experiment, you'll soon learn what works and what doesn't.

Gingered Stir-Fry

2" / 4cm piece fresh ginger root, chopped and crushed
2 cloves garlic, crushed
4 tablespoons / 60ml corn or sunflower oil
1 tablespoon / 15ml cornflour
small broccoli cut into small florets
5 ozs / 140g mange tout
1 large carrot cut into strips
4ozs / 115g small green beans topped and tailed
1 small onion, chopped
3 tablespoons tamari or shoyu
3 tablespoons water
salt and pepper to taste

Mix the ginger, garlic, cornflour and half of the oil in a large bowl until a paste is formed. Add the vegetables and mix well to coat them in the paste. Stir-fry the coated vegetables in the rest of the oil on a high heat for a few minutes, until the vegetables reach the consistency you prefer. Add the tamari, water, salt and pepper. Stir over a high heat, then reduce the heat, cover the pan and cook for a further 5 – 10 minutes.

Chickpea Stir-Fry   * FAT FREE *

4 tablespoons / 60ml water
4 tablespoons / 60ml lemon juice
2 cloves garlic, crushed
6 spring onions cut into small pieces
1 teaspoon dried mixed herbs
pinch of chilli powder
2 courgettes, sliced
1 large carrot, sliced thinly
12ozs / 350g broccoli florets, sliced thinly
1 x 14oz / 400g tin chickpeas, drained
2 tablespoons / 30ml tomato puree
salt and pepper to taste

Put the water and lemon juice in a wok and add the garlic, spring onions, herbs and chilli powder. Cook on a fairly low heat until the liquid has evaporated and the onions are beginning to soften. Add the courgette, carrot, broccoli and chickpeas and stir-fry for 5 minutes on high heat, stirring constantly. If the vegetables start to burn add a little more water.

Add the tomato puree, salt and pepper and stir in. Cover the pan and leave on very low heat for a further five minutes.

Hawaiian Stir-Fry * FAT FREE *

1 x 14oz / 400g tin pineapple chunks in their own juice, or use a small fresh pineapple cut into cubes
2 tablespoons / 30ml tamari or shoyu
3 cloves garlic, crushed
6 ozs /175g mange tout
4 ozs / 115g frozen peas
4 ozs / 115g small green beans, sliced lengthways
9 ozs / 250 g firm tofu, cubed
Salt and pepper to taste
1 teaspoon of Chinese 5-spice mixture

Drain the juice from the pineapples and put into a wok with the tamari. Add the pineapple chunks and everything except the 5-spice. Cook on high heat stirring constantly for 5 minutes – add a little water if it gets too dry.

Add the 5-spice and mix well. Cover the wok, turn the heat down low and leave for a further five minutes.

Runner Beans and Peanut Gravy

Gravy:
8oz / 225g smooth peanut butter
1 tablespoon / 15ml cornflour
1" / 2cm piece of root ginger, crushed
4 cloves garlic, crushed
Pinch of chilli powder
½ pint / 300ml water

Stir Fry:
1½ lb / 675g runner beans, cut into 1" / 2cm lengths
1 large courgette, cut into matchsticks
1 onion sliced thinly
1lb / 450g cauliflower in small florets
Water

Mix all the gravy ingredients in a blender until smooth.

Place the vegetables in a wok and add ¼ pint / 150ml of water. Stir-fry on a moderate heat, adding more water if necessary, until the vegetables are tender. Add the gravy, mix it in and simmer gently for five minutes, stirring occasionally to avoid sticking.

Sabina Chance

BABY BAKING POTATOES

Baby Baking Potatoes

Things to do with baby potatoes

Most of this book is about the traditional baked potato, you know the ones that are large and with the addition of a suitable filling make a complete meal on their own. Recently there has emerged a different kind of baking potato – the baby baking potato. These are usually sold in plastic cartons in supermarkets and are of particular varieties that are good to bake when small.

Personally, over the years, I've often used small potatoes, usually when the kitchen is devoid of large ones or time for cooking is at a premium. They don't have to be labelled as baking potatoes, almost any variety will do; just pick those with nice clean skins that are firm and fresh. You can prepare these potatoes in exactly the same way as their larger cousins except they will need a shorter cooking time.

Sometimes I put five or six of them on a metal kebab skewer before putting them in the oven; this provides an ample meal for one with the addition of half a can of baked beans or some leftovers from last night's curry.

Here are some other suggestions that range from the prosaic to the gourmet. In some of these recipes the term 'baked' is only loosely applied.

"Roasted Baked" Potatoes and vegetables

1½ lb / 675g baby baking potatoes, cleaned and cut in half lengthways
3 carrots cut into 2" / 4cm long batons
1 red pepper sliced
1 large courgette cut into batons
8 oz / 225g mushrooms, sliced
1 large leek sliced
5 cloves of garlic crushed
4 tablespoons / 60ml extra virgin olive oil
2 teaspoons / 10ml dried oregano
salt and pepper to taste

Mix all the ingredients in a large deep oven tray until everything is thinly coated in oil, finally placing the potatoes cut side down. Put the tray, uncovered, in a hot oven, 225 degrees C and cook for 45 minutes or until the potatoes are cooked.

Baby Baker and Butter Bean Casserole

2 lbs / 900g of baby baking potatoes, scrubbed and cleaned.
2 onions sliced
4 cloves garlic sliced thinly
1 leek sliced
1 green chilli deseeded and chopped
½ lb / 225g green beans washed and cut into 1" / 2cm strips
4 tablespoons / 60ml olive oil
Juice of half a lemon
Salt and pepper to taste
1 teaspoon / 5ml of mixed herbs
1 x 14 oz / 400g tin cooked butter beans

Put the potatoes, onions, garlic, leek, chilli and green beans in a deep casserole or oven dish and drizzle over a generous amount of olive oil. Add the lemon juice, salt, pepper and herbs and mix well.

Cover the dish and place in the centre of a hot oven, 225 degrees C for at least an hour. Remove the dish from the oven, add the cooked butter beans and their juice and mix again. Return to the oven, cover and cook for another 20 minutes

Vegetable Medley and Baby Potatoes

2lbs / 900g baby baking potatoes scrubbed and cleaned
2 carrots cut into small chunks
½ lb / 225g French beans washed and sliced
12 ozs / 350g pumpkin or squash cubed
1 onion chopped roughly
6 ozs / 175g button mushrooms washed and halved
2 cloves garlic, crushed
1 x 14oz / 400g tin of chopped tomatoes
1 teaspoon / 5ml paprika
1 teaspoon / 5ml dried parsley
salt and pepper to taste
4 tablespoons / 60ml sunflower oil

Mix all the ingredients thoroughly in a deep casserole or oven dish, cover and cook at 200 degrees C for 1½ hours.

Tofu and Olive Baby Baker Feast

2lbs / 900g baby baking potatoes scrubbed and cleaned
9 ozs / 250g firm tofu cut in ½" / 1cm cubes
5 ozs / 140g pitted black olives
8 ozs / 225g green beans, topped and tailed only
8 ozs / 225g button mushrooms, cut in halves
8 ozs / 225g carrots sliced
1 green pepper sliced
1 large onion sliced
2 green chillies chopped
5 cloves garlic crushed
1 x 14oz / 400g tin drained red kidney beans
5 tablespoons / 75ml extra virgin olive oil

Mix everything in a large casserole / oven dish, cover and cook for 2 hours at 200 degrees C.

SAUCES AND EXTRAS

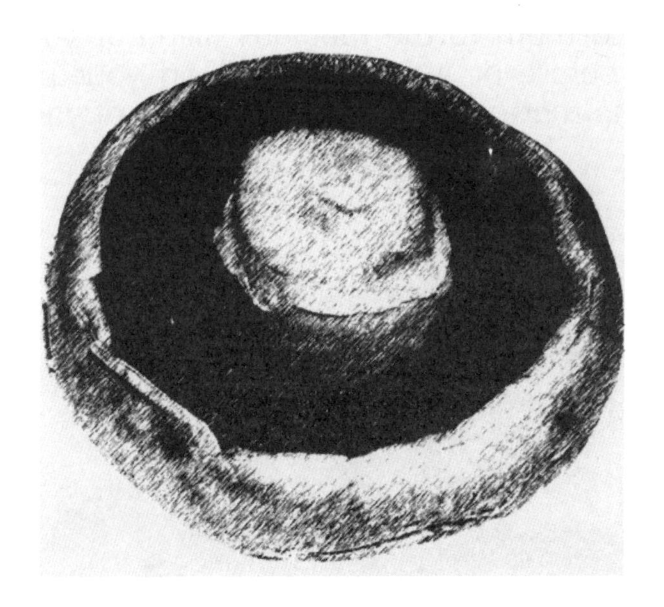

Sauces and Extras

Jazz it up – Sauces and extras to give your potato that extra punch.

Sometimes, potatoes can seem a little dry without a dollop of margarine, but why not try some of these sauces or other extra ingredients that can turn a baked potato into a gourmet feast.

Just add them to the fabulous filling of your choice either before or after putting it on your potato, or combine them to make unique fillings of your own.

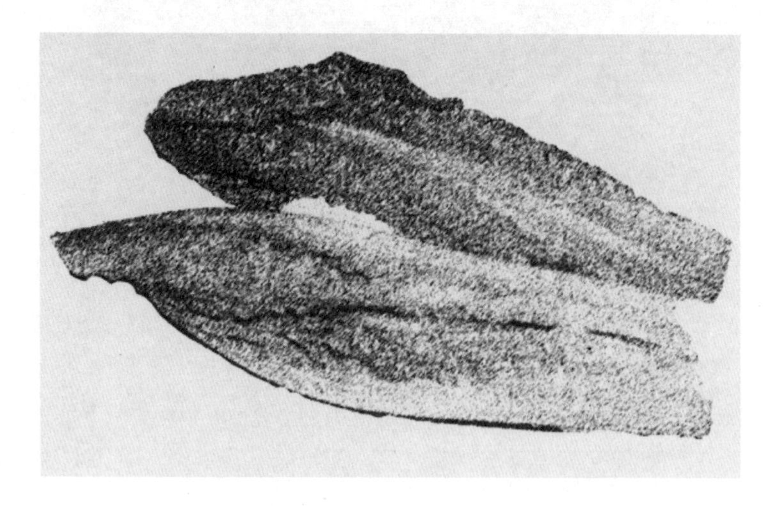

Tahini and Tamari

Mix a couple of teaspoons / 10ml of tamari or shoyu soya sauce with a generous dollop of tahini; add a few drops of water and some freshly ground black pepper. Whisk with a fork and spoon over potatoes.

Mushroom Gravy

4 tablespoons / 60ml vegetable oil
1 medium onion, chopped finely
2 cloves garlic, crushed
4 ozs / 115g mushrooms, sliced very thinly
4 heaped tablespoons / 60ml white flour
1 pint / 600ml prepared vegetable stock or water
1 level teaspoon / 5ml yeast extract
2 teaspoons / 10ml tamari or shoyu
Salt and pepper

Sauté the onion and garlic in the oil, in a large frying pan until soft and translucent. Add the chopped mushrooms and continue frying. Add the flour and cook for a few minutes without burning the flour. Add the stock gradually until the desired consistency is reached. Boiling water can be used instead of stock. Add the yeast extract and the soy sauce to taste. Season with the salt and pepper if needed.

Hot and Cold Salsa Sauce

Mix one 14oz / 400g tin of chopped tomatoes with 4 finely chopped chillies, 1 finely chopped raw onion and a pinch of salt.

Grated Cheezly

It's a branded product but it's impossible to replicate yourself so buy a pack of Cheddar style Cheezly from a health food shop, grate it through a cheese grater and add it to your lovely fluffy potato.

Peanut Sauce

1 onion, chopped
1 red chilli chopped
small piece of root ginger crushed
1 tablespoon / 15ml vegetable oil
2 tablespoons / 30ml cornflour
½ pint / 300ml pineapple juice
3 tablespoons / 45ml tamari or shoyu soya sauce
7 ozs / 200g crunchy peanut butter

Fry the onion, chilli and ginger in the oil until the onion starts to soften. Add the cornflour and stir. Add the pineapple juice a little at a time, stirring to stop burning and to mix well. Add the soya sauce and stir. Add the peanut butter and continue to heat gently while stirring for 5 minutes.

Simple Tomato Sauce

Fry a chopped onion with 2 crushed cloves of garlic. Add a tin of tomatoes and half a tube of tomato puree. Bring to the boil and then simmer gently for 10 minutes, stirring occasionally.

Season with salt and black pepper.

Cheddar Cheese Style Sauce

1 onion chopped finely
2 cloves garlic crushed
3 tablespoons / 45ml sunflower oil
4 tablespoons / 60ml white flour
½ pint / 300ml water
½ pint / 300ml soya milk
5 oz / 140g grated cheddar style Cheezly
Salt and pepper to taste

Fry the onion and garlic in the oil until soft, add the flour and cook and stir until a thick paste is formed. Add the liquid gradually, stirring constantly as it heats up. When it reaches the right consistency add the Cheezly, salt and pepper and stir in.

Bacon Style Pieces

6 fluid ozs / 175ml water
2 tablespoons / 30ml vegetable oil
5 tablespoons / 75ml tamari
1 tablespoon / 15ml sugar
3 cloves garlic, minced
5 ozs / 140g (dry weight) TVP savoury mince

Put all the ingredients in a saucepan, bring to the boil, remove from the heat, cover and leave to cool and absorb all the liquid. Spread the TVP on a baking tray lightly coated in oil. Bake in a preheated oven (180 degrees C) for 15 – 20 minutes turning once halfway through cooking. Remove from the oven and leave to cool. Store in a glass jar and use as sprinkles on your delicious baked potatoes.

Slow Roasted Aubergines and Courgettes

1 large aubergine, sliced into rounds
6 courgettes, sliced into rounds
6 tablespoons / 90ml olive oil
4 tablespoons / 60ml balsamic vinegar
1 teaspoon / 5ml salt

Mix all the ingredients in an oven tray. Place in a low oven – 120 degrees centigrade for 3 – 4 hours, turning occasionally. If they cook too fast, turn the heat down a bit.

These can be stored in jars in the fridge and brought to the table as needed.

Plamil Egg Free Mayonnaise

Another brand but again very difficult to substitute with home made. You can try the recipe below, it's lovely in its own way.

Mock Mayonnaise

½ pint / 275ml soya milk, few drops of ready made mustard, 1 tablespoon / 15ml lemon juice, pinch of salt, pinch of paprika, 3 tablespoons / 45ml sunflower oil

Mix all the ingredients, except the oil, in a blender. Add the oil a bit at a time and continue to blend until the desired consistency is reached.

Marinated Tofu Strips

Take a 9oz / 250g block of firm tofu, rinse it and drain it. Slice it into thin strips about 1" / 2cm wide. Spread the tofu on a plate and shake plenty of strong soya sauce (preferably tamari) over it. Add grated ginger and chopped chillies for a more spicy taste. Leave the tofu in the marinade until as much as possible has been absorbed (up to an hour), turning occasionally to coat it evenly.

Fry in olive oil on both sides until it's a nice golden brown and the edges are starting to crisp.

Yummy!

Baked Beans

The classic baked potato filling; simply open a can of your favourite baked beans, heat and pour over the potato.

Or get your baked beans bouncing by adding one or two tablespoons / 15 – 30ml of ready-made curry powder to the beans before heating them up.

Tomato Salad

Slice 2 lbs / 900g of tomatoes and mix with 6 tablespoons / 90ml olive oil, 2 tablespoons / 30ml balsamic vinegar and a teaspoon of salt. Let to stand at room temperature for an hour and a half.

Onion Bhajee Bits

8 ozs / 225g Gram flour
1 teaspoon / 5ml salt
3 tablespoons / 45ml curry powder
1 tablespoon / 15ml caraway seeds
½ pint / 300ml cold water
1 ½ lbs / 675g onions, sliced thinly
Cooking oil for deep frying

Sieve the gram flour, salt and curry powder into a large mixing bowl and add the caraway seeds. Mix well, Make a well in the centre and add cold water, bit by bit. Mix with a wooden spoon into a thick batter. Leave to stand whilst preparing the onions. Peel the onions and cut them into quarters. Slice them thinly. Add the onions to the batter and mix until they are all well coated with the batter.

Heat a deep fat fryer to 190 degrees C. Spoon the mixture into the hot oil, stir to separate and fry until golden brown and crisp, stirring now and again to break them up. Remove with a slotted spoon and serve over potato.

Mustardy Grated Carrot

Put 2 teaspoons / 10ml of mustard seed, yellow or black, in a hot dry frying pan and stir until they start to pop. Add the seeds to 1 lb / 450g of grated carrots, the juice of two lemons, a teaspoon / 5ml of salt and a bunch of chopped basil or mint leaves.

Marinated Mushrooms

Mix half a pound / 225g of sliced mushrooms with 5fl ozs / 150 ml of olive oil, a tablespoon / 15ml of soya sauce, a few sprigs of chopped parsley, 2 cloves of crushed garlic and some freshly ground black pepper. Let it all stand in the fridge for an hour or two before serving.

Cold Bean Salad

Mix together the following ingredients:

Butter beans, chick peas and kidney beans in equal proportions
1 red or green pepper chopped finely
A small tin of sweetcorn
As many chopped black olives as you can tolerate
4 tablespoons / 60ml olive oil
2 tablespoons / 30ml cider vinegar
1 teaspoon / 5ml of salt
A few twists of freshly ground black pepper

Let it all stand in the fridge for an hour. Serve.

Walberg Salad and Dressing

Salad:
1 Medium size iceberg lettuce, shredded
1 or 2 Cox apples, cut into small slices
1 or 2 red onions, sliced thinly
5ozs / 140g walnuts, broken into small pieces

Dressing:
3 tablespoons / 45ml sunflower oil
2 tablespoons / 30ml white wine vinegar
1 - 2 teaspoons / 5ml – 10ml prepared mustard
salt to taste

Put the ingredients for the dressing in a screw top jar and shake well.

Mix the salad ingredients in a bowl with the dressing. Leave covered in a refrigerator for at least an hour. Mix again before serving.

Garlic Mushrooms

1lb / 450g mushrooms, washed and halved
6 cloves garlic crushed
2 ozs / 55g margarine or 4 tablespoons olive oil
salt and pepper to taste

Put everything in a casserole dish. Put a lid on it and bake in a hot oven for 30 minutes. Alternatively, fry gently for 20 minutes in a covered pan.

Crunchy Salad with Walnuts

½ an iceberg lettuce, shredded
small cos lettuce, shredded
1 large carrot, grated
2 sticks celery, cut into ½" / 1cm pieces
1 green pepper, cut into strips 1" x ¼" / 2cm x 5mm
8ozs / 225g fresh Beansprouts
2 spring onions, cut into ½" / 1cm pieces
3 tablespoons / 45ml pumpkin seeds
3 ozs / 85g pitted black olives, cut in half
4ozs / 115g broken up walnuts
Juice of one lemon
2 tablespoons / 30ml olive oil
Salt and freshly ground black pepper to taste

Mix all the ingredients thoroughly in a large bowl. Set aside in the refrigerator for at least half an hour before serving.

Goes well with Plamil Egg Free Mayonnaise

Hummous

1 x 14oz / 400g can cooked chickpeas including liquid
6oz / 175g tahini
2 cloves garlic
juice of 1 lemon
1 teaspoon / 5ml salt
2 tablespoons / 30ml olive oil
water if necessary

Grind all the ingredients until a thick creamy paste is formed. You may need to add a little water if it's too stiff.

You may want to use just one clove of garlic if you don't like it to taste too strong.

Sabina Chance

GLOSSARY

Glossary

Some of the ingredients and terms you may not be familiar with.

Aduki Beans
(or Adzuki Beans)

These small red beans originate from China and are especially rich and savoury when cooked well. Like most beans they are very good in nutritional value.

They are not widely available but it's worth seeking them out. After soaking them overnight they should be cooked for up to an hour.

Blackeye Beans

Sometimes called Black Eye Peas, these are small cream coloured beans with a distinctive 'black eye'. They are quick to cook and have a pleasant nutty taste and a smooth texture.

Borlotti Beans

The Borlotti bean is used extensively in Italy and is a soft brown in colour with darker coloured streaks. They are available dried or pre-cooked in cans. In America they are sometimes referred to as Cranberry Beans.

Butter Beans

These are large cream-coloured, kidney-shaped beans available dried or cooked in cans. They can be cooked and mashed into a puree as well as forming the basis of many bean-based dishes.

Cheezly

Is dairy, lactose and gluten free and is made from potato starch, vegetable oil and soya protein. The 'Cheddar Style' variety is a bona fide alternative to cheddar cheese and can be used in cooking just like 'normal' cheese.

The Redwood Wholefood Company who make Cheezly also make it in different variations including a delicious Mozzarella style that melts wonderfully on your baked potato.

Chinese 5-spice

This is a mixture of 5 spices commonly used in Chinese style cooking. It normally consists of a mixture of ground cinnamon, peppercorns, star anise, fennel and cloves.

Discovery Refried Beans

These are a brand of refried beans that contain a very well balanced mix of spices so that when added to a dish, no other seasoning is normally required. See Refried Beans

Dried Beans

All beans are from the legume family; these are a class of plants that grow pods that contain seeds. These seeds include beans, peas and lentils.

The beans are dried and then packaged for sale in supermarkets and health food shops. Most shops carry only a limited range of beans; the best place to find the widest range is in wholefood shops and some health food shops.

Dried beans need to be soaked in water, usually at least overnight before use. Some dried beans then need to be boiled rapidly for at least ten minutes to remove possible toxins.

Before cooking in fresh water the beans should be rinsed thoroughly to reduce their renowned 'gas-giving' properties.

Garbanzo Beans

Another name for Chickpeas.

Garam Masala

A blend of spices commonly used in Indian cooking, similar to curry powder but often added at the end of cooking to produce an aromatic finish.

The blend of spices varies for different brands but usually includes cardamom, coriander seeds and cloves amongst others.

Ghee

Traditionally made from butter that has been heat treated to remove the solids so that it can be heated to a higher temperature without smoking.

Now available derived from vegetable fats.

Gram Flour

Gram flour is available from some supermarkets, health food stores and shops selling Asian produce. It is usually made from ground up chickpeas. One of its main uses is in Onion Bhajees and other Indian fritter type dishes.

Moong dhal

Refers to the small yellow lentils you can buy in some supermarkets and in shops that sell Asian produce. Moong dhal cooks quickly because of its small size and needs no pre-soaking.

Parmazano

Is a dairy free alternative to grated parmesan cheese. It is made chiefly from soya bean flour and palm oil. It can be used to give your baked potato an extra hit of flavour, especially when served with tomato based toppings.

Pinto Beans

These are a medium sized bean speckled with brown and cream. They are used in Mexican cooking and are usually the main ingredient of refried beans

Plamil Egg Free Mayonnaise

A non-animal substitute for traditional egg mayonnaise. Made with sunflower oil and pea protein. Adds a sharp creaminess to your baked potato.

Potato

The main subject of this book, Latin name *Solanum Tuberosum*. Potatoes are tubers or growths on the roots of the potato plant, a native of South America, now used extensively all over the world.

Red Kidney Beans

Largish red kidney shaped beans, (also available in black), very commonly used in chillies and mixed bean salads.

Refried Beans

Refers to a type of beans used in Mexican cooking. They are usually cooked and mashed Pinto Beans that are then fried with onion and other spices.

Salsa

Salsa is another food often used in Mexico and is made from chopped tomatoes mixed with chillies onions, peppers and sometimes other ingredients. Depending on the level of spices used Salsa can be very 'hot'. Usually served cold from the fridge.

Seitan

Can be purchased in some health food shops in tins or jars. It's made from wheat gluten and is high in protein.

Shoyu

Is a dark soya sauce made from fermenting soya beans and wheat. It tastes salty and can be used to add flavour to almost any dish. See Tamari.

Tahini

Made from crushed sesame seeds and nothing else. It can take a little while to get used to because of its dry taste, but if you add a few drops of tamari or yeast extract, it can make a nice savoury sauce for your potato.

Tamari

True soya sauce, made by fermenting soya beans with rice. Similar to Shoyu but no wheat, hence gluten free, and it is a little stronger tasting. See Shoyu

Tofu

Is made by heating soya milk with a coagulant to form 'curds' which are then pressed to release the moisture and firm the tofu up. It is available in several different forms, most notably silken tofu and firm tofu. Firm tofu can be marinated in tamari and deep-fried to provide a very savoury bite that can be added to a wide range of dishes.

Tofu originated in China at least 2000 years ago and is one of the staple foods of much of rural China.

TVP

TVP or Textured Vegetable Protein is made from defatted soya flour. It is usually flavoured and dried then added to dishes to give a high protein boost and a chewy texture.

TVP usually comes in mince form that is re-hydrated and used in dishes like Bolognese.

TVP Chunks are also available which are about 1cm cubes that can be re-hydrated and added to curries and savoury dishes to give a chunky, chewy bite.

TVP is sometimes fortified with vitamin B12.

Vegan

A vegan is a person who does not consume any animal products at all. Surprisingly to some the foods that vegans avoid include honey and eggs as well as cheese and all dairy products.

Vegetarian

A vegetarian is a person who does not consume any animals, as opposed to animal products. Vegetarians will eat foods derived from cow's or other animal's milk and they will usually eat eggs.

Vegetarians do not eat fish either.

Sabina Chance

INDEX

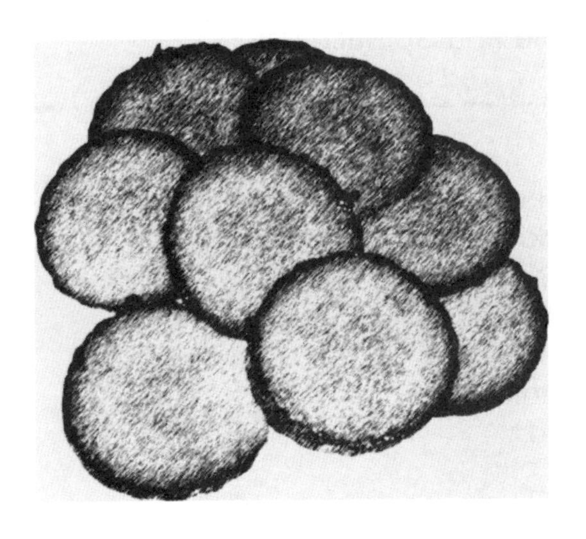

Index

P

Q

R

S

T

V

W

About Opening Chapter

Opening Chapter is a publisher that likes to take a fresh approach to publishing. We develop titles that offer that little bit extra.

The titles that we publish are diverse and different, but we never compromise on quality.

Please keep a look out for our books; you won't be disappointed.

On the following pages are extracts from some forthcoming titles to give you a taste of what we have to offer.

Thank you.

Super Soups and Stews by Sabina Chance
(suitable for vegetarians and vegans)

To be published late summer 2005

Extract from Super Soups and Stews.:
'CREAMY' MUSHROOM SOUP

12ozs / 400g mushrooms, sliced and chopped into small pieces
1 pint / 600ml soya milk
1 pint / 600ml of water
1 tablespoon / 15ml of finely chopped fresh parsley
1½ ozs / 40g soya margarine
3 tablespoons / 45ml of unbleached white flour
Salt and pepper to taste

Put the mushrooms and the water into a saucepan, bring to boil and simmer for a few minutes. Strain the mushrooms and set aside, keep the stock. Melt the margarine in a large saucepan and stir in the flour and cook gently for a few minutes until a smooth paste is formed.

Keep the pan on the heat and add the mushroom stock and the soya milk to the flour a little at a time stirring continuously to avoid lumps. Add the chopped parsley and the seasonings and simmer for 10 minutes stirring occasionally to avoid sticking.

Add the cooked mushrooms and adjust the seasoning to taste. Reheat the soup but do not boil. Serve immediately. If you want a 'creamier' soup stir in some soya cream before serving.

The Three Bears

A novel by Derec Jones exploring the inner and outer life of the unnamed narrator in a way that will challenge your perceptions of the physical universe in which we live.

To be published late 2005

Extract From The Three Bears:

It's done now – the ceiling, all but done anyway. It still needs a coat or two of varnish and maybe a bit of wood filler here and there – where the knots have fallen out, but otherwise it's done. The rest of the kitchen's the same; it's all just about done. That's me all over, just about done, I can never seem to finish a job, perhaps I'm afraid that if I ever do then I'll be done too. There's always some unresolved business, unrealised potential, I always hold something back, something substantial. Why can't I give? I ask her.

"Why can't some people change?"

"Change?"

"Why is it that some, most, people don't like dramatic change in their lives? What are they afraid of?"

"You're not going on about that again are you?"

"No, no, I'm just being philosophical, just theorising, you know, imagining."

"Yeah well, I'm tired of it all."

"But things have to change, everything changes, nothing lasts forever."

"What about diamonds?"

"I don't know. I suppose even diamonds get

crushed to atoms, even atoms get crushed to subatomic particles, if they go into a Black Hole that is."

"There's only one thing for it then."

"Oh yeah. What's that?"

"I thought you knew everything."

"Oh well, if you can't be bothered. If all you want to do is take the piss . . ."

"You're so precious, you know that. So bloody precious. Why can't you just get on with it like everyone else has to?"

"Hang on, this isn't meant to be an argument, I was just thinking that's all."

"That's all you ever do. It's no good for you, thinking too much, why can't you just enjoy life? Why can't you just be happy? What's the point of all this doom and gloom?"

"It's not doom and gloom, I'm not freaked out or depressed or anything. I just like to look behind things, work out what's going on, that sort of thing."

"Start a religious bloody cult or something then. Yes, go on, start a cult and then you can go and live with your followers in some American desert or something and then you can talk bollocks all you like, but I'm just tired of it all. All I want is to do my job and have a good time now and again."

"What's up with you?"

"What do you mean?"

"What's really up with you? What's going on?"

"Oh, I don't know. I'm sorry. I didn't mean to snap."

"Come here."

We hug, but I'm not sure if she really wants to or she just wants to shut me up. I get the feeling that she's making a face over my shoulder, like they do in soap operas, so that the audience get to know something the characters don't. I'm getting to feel more like a character in a soap opera all the time lately, what with cheap video cameras and infestations of CCTV everywhere you go. Maybe I'm watching too much telly?

After a decent interval where we just make a meal together and discuss only banal things like how many carrots to chop up for the aduki bean pie, or whether to use olive oil or sunflower oil to sauté the onions and garlic in, I tell her about the woman copper who came around to see me yesterday.

"Why?" She asks. "Why are they still bothering you?"

. . . .

The Walker and other Stories

A collection of short stories that sometimes take a different perspective on life on this planet. Each story is like an iceberg, there's a lot going on beneath the surface.

To be published early 2006

Extract from The Walker and other Stories.

From "The Richest Man in the World"

I am the richest man in the world. I am a recluse. I am afraid of doorknobs. I shower in purified water a dozen times a day. I eat nothing but the flesh of sterilised fruit. It's true; I am the richest man in the world, the rest doesn't matter, it's of no consequence, it's irrelevant. All that matters is that these words reach you, that we touch.

I have no one you see – no mother, no father, no wife, no sons, no daughters, no family, no friends - oh! I have slaves, paid slaves, unpaid sycophants, admirers, devotees even. I suspect that every minute of every day my name is on the lips of someone; my name is typed into a word-processor; my name is faxed at the speed of light.

I live at a secret address in the city of London; from the outside, it merges into the streets, just another run-down multi-occupancy property. Inside, it's different - my private heaven, my private hell. I won't tell you where it is, you'll only tell the press, then I'll be besieged by hordes of desperate reporters with cameras and stupid questions. I'll be digested, twisted, corrupted, and regurgitated in little boxes, neatly wrapped and categorised, another item on the shelves of the super-psyche-market to be picked up, examined, eaten and defecated.

Aeons ago, in another life, I came from the swamps, just like you, fought for air until my lungs grew, shook the mud from my webbed feet and rolled in the sun on the damp grass. I lifted my eyes to the moon and the stars, and cried like a wolf. I fashioned a stick of wood and dug out the sweet bodies of ants.

I shouted and screamed and laughed in the rain and danced on the graves of my enemies. I worshipped a God, I sucked a breast, I ran with the wind.

The streets of the city welcomed me, they bruised me and cut me, they fed me until they owned me. I learnt how to play their games, how to juggle their balls, how to hedge my bets, and eventually I won. I started to win and never stopped, now I have no need to play. The process is automatic, every day the treasures pour into my coffers like pins flying to a magnet, like water to the sea. I am the sea.

On the streets of the city, I am the dreamer, nothing will hurt me, it's under my control. I succumb to the dream. A bench in a park, I have nothing.

"Bit cold today mate! Bet you wish you'd worn a coat?"

"What? - cold, coat? Yes, you're right."

"Nice weather for the time of year though, innit?"

"Suppose so."

"Ere, fancy a drink mate? Warm you up, a nice tot of whisky or something?" . . . .

The Words in Me

A collection of poetry that explores the form in surprising ways; challenging but always accessible, this book brings the words we all use alive to form *"a new reality"*

To be published Summer 2005

Extract from The Words in Me

On Walls

On walls
low brick walls
boys sit
and think
boys spit
and cover the tarmac
with white globules

In their rooms
they keep grime
proddable stuff
dark places
to hide futures